The bond child brought to the test; and his use of the letter considered. By William Huntington, S.S.

William Huntington

Eighteenth Century
Collections Online
Print Editions

Gale ECCO Print Editions

Relive history with *Eighteenth Century Collections Online*, now available in print for the independent historian and collector. This series includes the most significant English-language and foreign-language works printed in Great Britain during the eighteenth century, and is organized in seven different subject areas including literature and language; medicine, science, and technology; and religion and philosophy. The collection also includes thousands of important works from the Americas.

The eighteenth century has been called "The Age of Enlightenment." It was a period of rapid advance in print culture and publishing, in world exploration, and in the rapid growth of science and technology – all of which had a profound impact on the political and cultural landscape. At the end of the century the American Revolution, French Revolution and Industrial Revolution, perhaps three of the most significant events in modern history, set in motion developments that eventually dominated world political, economic, and social life.

In a groundbreaking effort, Gale initiated a revolution of its own: digitization of epic proportions to preserve these invaluable works in the largest online archive of its kind. Contributions from major world libraries constitute over 175,000 original printed works. Scanned images of the actual pages, rather than transcriptions, recreate the works *as they first appeared.*

Now for the first time, these high-quality digital scans of original works are available via print-on-demand, making them readily accessible to libraries, students, independent scholars, and readers of all ages.

For our initial release we have created seven robust collections to form one the world's most comprehensive catalogs of 18th century works.

Initial Gale ECCO Print Editions collections include:

History and Geography
Rich in titles on English life and social history, this collection spans the world as it was known to eighteenth-century historians and explorers. Titles include a wealth of travel accounts and diaries, histories of nations from throughout the world, and maps and charts of a world that was still being discovered. Students of the War of American Independence will find fascinating accounts from the British side of conflict.

Social Science

Delve into what it was like to live during the eighteenth century by reading the first-hand accounts of everyday people, including city dwellers and farmers, businessmen and bankers, artisans and merchants, artists and their patrons, politicians and their constituents. Original texts make the American, French, and Industrial revolutions vividly contemporary.

Medicine, Science and Technology

Medical theory and practice of the 1700s developed rapidly, as is evidenced by the extensive collection, which includes descriptions of diseases, their conditions, and treatments. Books on science and technology, agriculture, military technology, natural philosophy, even cookbooks, are all contained here.

Literature and Language

Western literary study flows out of eighteenth-century works by Alexander Pope, Daniel Defoe, Henry Fielding, Frances Burney, Denis Diderot, Johann Gottfried Herder, Johann Wolfgang von Goethe, and others. Experience the birth of the modern novel, or compare the development of language using dictionaries and grammar discourses.

Religion and Philosophy

The Age of Enlightenment profoundly enriched religious and philosophical understanding and continues to influence present-day thinking. Works collected here include masterpieces by David Hume, Immanuel Kant, and Jean-Jacques Rousseau, as well as religious sermons and moral debates on the issues of the day, such as the slave trade. The Age of Reason saw conflict between Protestantism and Catholicism transformed into one between faith and logic -- a debate that continues in the twenty-first century.

Law and Reference

This collection reveals the history of English common law and Empire law in a vastly changing world of British expansion. Dominating the legal field is the *Commentaries of the Law of England* by Sir William Blackstone, which first appeared in 1765. Reference works such as almanacs and catalogues continue to educate us by revealing the day-to-day workings of society.

Fine Arts

The eighteenth-century fascination with Greek and Roman antiquity followed the systematic excavation of the ruins at Pompeii and Herculaneum in southern Italy; and after 1750 a neoclassical style dominated all artistic fields. The titles here trace developments in mostly English-language works on painting, sculpture, architecture, music, theater, and other disciplines. Instructional works on musical instruments, catalogs of art objects, comic operas, and more are also included.

The BiblioLife Network

This project was made possible in part by the BiblioLife Network (BLN), a project aimed at addressing some of the huge challenges facing book preservationists around the world. The BLN includes libraries, library networks, archives, subject matter experts, online communities and library service providers. We believe every book ever published should be available as a high-quality print reproduction; printed on-demand anywhere in the world. This insures the ongoing accessibility of the content and helps generate sustainable revenue for the libraries and organizations that work to preserve these important materials.

The following book is in the "public domain" and represents an authentic reproduction of the text as printed by the original publisher. While we have attempted to accurately maintain the integrity of the original work, there are sometimes problems with the original work or the micro-film from which the books were digitized. This can result in minor errors in reproduction. Possible imperfections include missing and blurred pages, poor pictures, markings and other reproduction issues beyond our control. Because this work is culturally important, we have made it available as part of our commitment to protecting, preserving, and promoting the world's literature.

GUIDE TO FOLD-OUTS MAPS and OVERSIZED IMAGES

The book you are reading was digitized from microfilm captured over the past thirty to forty years. Years after the creation of the original microfilm, the book was converted to digital files and made available in an online database.

In an online database, page images do not need to conform to the size restrictions found in a printed book. When converting these images back into a printed bound book, the page sizes are standardized in ways that maintain the detail of the original. For large images, such as fold-out maps, the original page image is split into two or more pages

Guidelines used to determine how to split the page image follows:

• Some images are split vertically; large images require vertical and horizontal splits.
• For horizontal splits, the content is split left to right.
• For vertical splits, the content is split from top to bottom.
• For both vertical and horizontal splits, the image is processed from top left to bottom right.

THE

BOND CHILD

BROUGHT TO THE *TEST*;

AND HIS

USE OF THE *LETTER* CONSIDERED.

BY

WILLIAM HUNTINGTON, S S.

WHO HATH MADE US ABLE MINISTERS OF THE NEW TESTAMENT;
NOT OF THE LETTER, BUT OF THE SPIRIT FOR THE LETTER
KILLETH, BUT THE SPIRIT GIVETH LIFE. 2 COR. III. 6.

LONDON:

Printed for G. Terry, Nº 54, Paternoster Row; J Davidson, Nº 7,
Postern Row, Tower Hill, and J Baker, Nº 226, Oxford Street;
where all Booksellers may be supplied Sold, also, at Providence
Chapel; and at Monkwell Street Meeting, every Tuesday Evening.

MDCCLXXXIX.

THE

B·OND CHILD

BROUGHT TO THE *TEST*, &c.

———————————

TO

MR. WAKE,

MINISTER OF THE LETTER,

AT SMARDEN, IN KENT.

SIR,

THE great apoſtle of the Gentiles tells us to beware of dogs, evil workers, and of the conciſion, or cutters, who, like poor Peter, take a carnal weapon, inſtead of a ſpiritual one, and cut at the high-prieſt's ſervant's ear, inſtead of the traitor's heart. You have been ſent for (by Mr. Stonehouſe) to Cranbrook, I find, the place of my nativity; and you have attempted, by a few of your own chimeras palmed upon the holy law of God, to ridicule, and bring into contempt, what I believe to be, the truths of the everlaſting Goſpel. " Mr. Stonehouſe, it ſeems, was too much taken up " in buſineſs; he wanted time:"—and, perhaps, he wants truth, and the power and experience of it, as

A 2   much

much as time.   Be that as it may, "*You would go*
"*home,*" as you expreſſed yourſelf, "*and rummage*
"*up all your lumber for the expedition,*" though you
was adviſed to the contrary.   Surely, if you had
been armed and equipped from Heaven, you would
have been fit for the field, without riding ſo many
miles to plunder the arguments of the dead.

You report   that you formerly attended Mr.
C.——n, to hear depths of doctrine, Mr. R———n,
to have your graces ſtirred up; and Mr. Huntington, to hear oddities: and I believe they are oddities,
and ever will remain ſo, to novices, for *the preach-*
ing of the croſs of Chriſt is, to them that periſh, fooliſh-
neſs.   But did not all theſe *depths, ſtirrings,* and
oddities, furniſh you for the attack?   Have you no
truth, nor arguments, but what lay on the ſhelves of
your ſtudy?   If the Spirit and Word of God had dwelt
in you, and if God had ſent you on this warfare,
he would have furniſhed you both with armour and
weapons.   A good ſoldier of Jeſus Chriſt is never
without his armour, nor his artillery; nor does he
go a warfare at his own expence.   *Fetching lumber*
from Smarden, plainly proves that God had no hand
in the expedition: beſides, arguments borrowed
from authors by graceleſs men are never forcible
ror want of a divine edge.   If *God be the ſword of a*
man's excellency, the excellency and power of God
will attend the man.   Without this, however fine
the reaſonings, however nice the diſtinctions, how-

ever

ever eloquent the language, the man can do no more than carnalize, legalize, or philofophize, the *difpenfation of the Spirit*; and the SOUL-BEGGARY of the man, whether he preach or write, will difcover itfelf, in all he fays or writes, to one who lives and walks in the Spirit of God. Many of our authors are not aware of this; they write and fpeak to difplay their abilities, and exalt themfelves in the eyes of others, and, when they have done all, it can only be called *the fpeech of them that are puffed up*, for there is no power; and, in truth, they only expofe their *pride* and *ignorance*, and the *ftarving condition* of their fouls; and convince the fpiritually-minded, that not a reformation in life, improvement in language, or even minifterial, which are called *fpiritual gifts*, make a man a fpiritual man. Nothing but a *fpiritual birth* can do this: *that which is born of the Spirit is fpirit.* Such men, though they may be ranked, as they often are by ignorant profeffors and weak believers, with *gofpel minifters*, yet neither their rank nor their gifts fecure heaven to them, nor their fouls from *falling headlong* into hell. *Judes* (fays Peter) *was* NUMBERED *with us, and had obtained part of this miniftry*, Acts i. 17. and it was the worft part, the *gift*, not the *grace*, that is fo neceffary for the difcharge of the office that he had taken: therefore from this *part* of the miniftry *Judas by tranfgreffion fell, that he might go to his own place.* This "coming and going from the place of
"the

" the holy will be eternally forgotten in the hea-
" venly Jerusalem," *Ecclef.* VIII. 10. though they
have so done in Mount Zion.

Nor did you *appear in well-set hair* at Cranbrook,
but in *baldnefs:* the *shame of your nakednefs* was not
hid, nor did your melody rise from the *certain found*
of the gospel-trumpet, but, like that of a *drum,*
from the *emptinefs* of the preacher.

Did God ever give you a meffage againft me?
Had you either your meffage or impulfe from him?
Did you once afk him either for matter or manner
in this undertaking? Did your face shine or heart
flow with grace in that *work of naught?* Did the
fair beauty of the Lord appear in the meeting?
Were the outgoings of God feen in it? or, " Did he
" once ftir up his ftrength, and come among you?"
Were the ungodly alarmed, the unruly warned, the
gainfayers confuted, the hypocrites expofed, and the
bowels of the faints refreshed? Did you go home
with the teftimony and approbation of God in your
heart? Had you nearnefs of accefs to him in prayer
at your return? or did either Scripture or Confcience
fay, *Well done, good and faithful fervant?* Don't
you think that the free-will Baptifts, the hypocriti-
cal Arminians, and fome that are called members of
that place, befide the openly profane, ftood in more
need of the sharpnefs that you ufed among them,
than I did? Is there one mote in my eye that the

beam

beam in your own will allow you to pull out? If there is, get about it.

Woe to such *wanton trifling!* Remember the fall of him that you are gone to succeed. I heard him, about twelve years ago, at Kingston upon Thames; and said, as soon as he had finished his discourse, that he had run before he was sent: and I said the same of one since, who was ordained at Hammer-smith, who confirmed me soon after, and the same of two since, whom God discovered in the same way—to let me know that my judgment of those men was from him. *Let him that thinketh he stand-eth, take heed left he fall.* I hope those who are going (according to report) to ordain you, will look about them, and *not lay hands suddenly on any man;* not countenance and recommend a man to the work of the ministry, upon a reason of his hope, and a confession of his faith, in general terms, without an account of his heart-felt experience of the truth; a confession of the faith delivered to him, and im-pressed on his foul, by God himself, and a testimony in the ordainers consciences from God, and from men of experience, touching the *testimony of God to the word of his grace* by him, besides the witness of some converts, or living seals of his mission and com-mission from God.

Sodomites, adulterers, and fornicators, have been palmed upon the church of God heretofore, instead of ministers of the Spirit. If he that *bids* an erroneous

man

man (who brings not the doctrine of Christ) *God speed*, is a partaker of his evil deeds; what must they be partakers of, who, upon a partial examination, a written school-boy's confession, and perhaps an unexperienced people's call, or an attachment to a party, *lay on hands*, countenance and send forth a wolf in sheep's cloathing, instead of an under-shepherd? It is well if this *work* does not one day recoil, with a double discharge both of grief and guilt, upon the consciences of many who in our day are called Presbyters. When God makes manifest the counsels of the heart, it will appear that this is no small part of *the mystery of spiritual wickedness*, (in the propagation of errors) that will be unfolded in the great day, to the confusion of Zion's deceitful workers and hypocrites, *who were before of old ordained to this condemnation*. Which pre-ordination of God is no excuse for a partial ordination by men.

I have not a single doubt of my effectual call, both to salvation and to the ministry of the everlasting gospel, and that by Jesus Christ himself: and I believe I may say that God has set his seal a thousand times to the ministry that I have received, by working a change in sinners hearts, and ministring the Spirit unto them   But, who sent you, I know not. Where is your genealogy? Where are the credentials that the Spirit of the living God has written on the fleshly tables of your heart? Produce the twofold witness, that of the Spirit, and of *conscience*, and the

mystery

myſtery of faith held therein. Let us have ſome
account of the ſigning and ſealing you to the day of
redemption, that we may know what image and
ſuperſcription you bear. If you are deſtitute of theſe
things, you run before you were ſent; and, if acquainted with them, (even but in theory) you ſin
againſt light and knowledge, by walking in crafti-
neſs, and handling the word of God deceitfully.

"The law is good, if a man uſe it lawfully."
I know it is: but, what could you bring from that
text againſt a man who loves the Lord Jeſus Chriſt
in ſincerity and truth? What is there in that paſſage
againſt one in covenant with God, under the dominion of grace, and that ſerves God in the newneſs of
the Spirit? *Is the law againſt the promiſe of God? God
forbid! The law is not made for a righteous man,
but for the lawleſs and diſobedient,* 1 Tim. i. 9.
"Whatſoever the law ſaith, it ſaith to them who are
"under the law." *Rom.* iii. 19. If the law is not
made for a righteous man, how could you apply it
to me, whom God has juſtified? and if what the Law
ſaith, it ſaith to them that are under it, how could
you level it's voice againſt them that are under
grace? The Law ſpeaks to ſuch as you, who ſeem
to be under it, and to them who are without the
law of faith, and diſobedient to the goſpel, called
lawleſs and diſobedient. But *they that are Chriſt's
have crucified the fleſh, with the affections and luſts;*

B   and

and *againſt ſuch there is no law,* Gal. v. 23, 24. What, then, could you make the Law, in your text, ſay againſt me?

The Law is handled lawfully when it is ſet forth as a tranſcript of the holineſs, truth, juſtice, immutability, and eternity, of God.

When it is ſet forth in the hand of Juſtice, accompanied with God's glittering ſword, in all it's ſpiritual meaning, and with all it's dreadful contents, againſt every ſinner that is out of Chriſt Jeſus, whether profeſſor or profane.

When it is preached as a revelation of the righteous judgments of God, a revelation of his juſt wrath and holy indignation againſt all ſin, and ſinners who are under the law, for they are under the curſe; and whatſoever things the Law ſaith, it ſaith to them.

It is handled lawfully when it's ſpiritual meaning is enforced, as reaching to the thoughts, words, works, and workings of the very ſouls of men; *working death in them by itſelf, which is good.*

It is handled lawfully when the eternity of it is inſiſted on; *ſo* that devils and damned ſouls ſhall have a gaol-delivery when God ſhall ceaſe to exiſt, when his eternal ſentence ſhall be recalled, and an everlaſting law be repealed—but not till then.

It is lawfully handled when it is ſet forth as added becauſe of tranſgreſſion, that ſin by the law might appear ſin, and become exceeding ſinful; that the offence might abound, being viewed in that perfect

glaſs;

glafs; that every mouth may be ftopped, and the whole world be brought in *guilty* before God.

It is handled lawfully when it is fet forth as magnified and made honourable by the Saviour, who gave a perfect obedience to every precept of it in his life; and was obedient to his Father in fubmitting to the fentence of it in death, even the death of the crofs.

When it is fet forth in the heart of Chrift, who is our Mercy-feat; and kept there, as the two tables of it were in the ark of old. And when it is enforced as written by God on the hearts of his people, and put into their minds; who caufes them to walk in his ftatutes, keep his judgments, and do them: fo that they are not without law to God, having it in their hearts; but under the law to Chrift, in whom the law of the Spirit of life makes them free from the law of fin and death.

Again, It is lawfully handled when it is proved that the end of the commandment is charity; that love is the fulfilling of the law, and that all thofe who have *laid hold on eternal life,* in whofe heart the love of God is fhed abroad, and to whofe faith the righteoufnefs of Chrift is imputed; *that the* RIGHTEOUSNESS *of the law is fulfilled in them, who walk not after the flefh, but after the Spirit.*

And it is lawfully handled by thofe who infift that the Chriftian loves the law of God after the inner man, and that with his mind he ferves the law of

God;

God; for the inner man has got the fubftance of the magnified law in him, and being written in the renewed mind, the renewed foul becomes a living epiftle, and the heavenly-minded Chriftian loves the law therewith: but, if you are a ftranger to this inner man, and to what Paul calls *renewing in the spirit of the mind*, you may, through the blindnefs and ignorance that is in you, call it Antinomianifm, and fo contemn the counfel of the Moft High, or darken it by words without knowledge, feeing thefe are things too wonderful for you, and things that you underftand not.

If a man fpeak, let him fpeak as the oracles of God, faith the Spirit; and I will leave you to judge whether the Law be not lawfully handled in this letter, and whether I have not fpoken in it agreeable to the oracles of God: and if, upon examination, you find I have, then in future ufe all the *lumber* that you may *rummage up*, againft the world, the flefh, and the devil; and leave me and my *oddities* to ftand or fall to my own Mafter. There is plenty of finners at Cranbrook to level your difcourfes at, without fpouting or bending your tongue (for lyes) at me; efpecially when you knew I was not prefent to anfwer for myfelf. If you will preach a difcourfe, and allow me to be prefent, I fhall have no objection to come down, and, if I cannot put you to fhame, you fhall put me to it. I have done nothing againft the truth, nor have I corrupted the word. Let us fee if you can fay the fame.

Your

Your text is—

" *The law is good if a man use it lawfully.*"
First, You endeavour'd to prove, " Who they were
" that used it lawfully. The unbeliever could not.
" *Ergo, it must be the believer.*"

" The believer having no more to do with the law
" than a woman with a dead husband, *is black Anti-*
" *nomianism.*"

" A non-entity may be a rule as soon as love."

" Faith is a hand, an eye, a leg—*Ergo*, no rule."

" The law is perfect, therefore, perpetual and
" everlasting."

" Angels are under it."

Is this speaking as the oracles of God? Let us try
it by *the law and the testimony if they speak not
according to this word, it is because there is no light
in them.*

" The unbeliever cannot use the law lawfully.
" Ergo, it must be the believer."

This, Sir, was as crafty a beginning as you could
make. It was right to put the unbeliever quite out
of the question, and then to introduce the believer,
as the only person that could make a lawful use of
the law, had the face of truth, and carried a very
fair shew with it, and, doubtless, this was as wise
a step as you could take to give your text a *deceitful
handling*, in order to blacken your antagonist, and
stumble the weak. But, though the context did not
answer

anſwer your end, it will anſwer mine, and therefore I ſhall produce it; and, without applying the words to unbelievers without reſtriction, I ſhall let them ſpeak to *ſuſpected teachers*, for to them they are directed, and eſpecially to *unbelieving*, or *faithleſs preachers, who run before they are ſent.*

" Timothy—As I beſought thee to abide ſtill at " Epheſus, when I went into Macedonia, that thou " mighteſt *charge ſome that they teach no other doc-* " *trine, neither give heed to fables, and endleſs gene-* " *alogies, which miniſter queſtions rather than godly* " *edifying which is in faith: ſo do.* Now the end " of the commandment is charity, out of a pure " heart, and of a good conſcience, and of faith " unfeigned; *from which ſome having ſwerved,* [or " *not aimed at*] have turned aſide to vain jangling; " *deſiring to be teachers of the law,* underſtanding " neither what they ſay nor whereof they affirm. " *But we know that the Law is good, if a man uſe it* " *lawfully.* Knowing this, that the Law is not made " for a righteous man, but for the lawleſs and diſ- " obedient." 1 *Tim.* Chap. i.

If you had handled this context faithfully, and levelled it's force againſt *miniſters of the letter,* and ſpoken from your text, as the *oracles of God,* againſt ſuch men, it would have eſtabliſhed my doctrine, and ſaved you the trouble of making application, for every new-born babe in the audience might have replied—*Thou art the man.* But applying it to
private

private believers inftead of public preachers, and ufing it as their *only rule of life,* inftead of ufing it as a charge to vain janglers, (who have fwerved from the faith) was the only method you could adopt in order to expofe your antagonift to contempt; and it is a method that fhall one day or other expofe you to it.

The end of the commandment is charity, out of a pure heart, a good confcience, and of faith unfeigned. He who is bleffed with this myftery, holds it faft, enjoys it, and preaches it; *is the real faint, and true fervant of Chrift;* and fuch a fervant is to charge fufpected perfons, that they preach no other doctrine; and they who fwerve, or aim not at this, are thofe that turn afide to vain jangling; novices, who *defire to be teachers of the Law, underftanding neither what they fay nor whereof they affirm.*

The Law is good if a man ufe it lawfully. Let us fee the lawful ufe that you have made of it. " The " unbeliever," you fay, " cannot ufe it lawfully." True: but, if you had made a lawful ufe of it, you fhould have levelled all it's contents at his head, for to him it belongs. " *Knowing*," fays Paul, " that the Law is made for the lawlefs and difobe- " dient." But you levelled all the *weighty matters* that you brought from it at me, who am a believer; *for I can fhew you my faith by my works,* and the Law is not made for a righteous man. If the unbeliever cannot make a lawful ufe of it, *ergo,* are
you

you not that unbeliever, and, through ignorance, have handled it unlawfully? And, if so, *ergo*, Who set such a novice at it? But, if malice led you thus to pervert the text knowingly, your sin is the greater, and such walking in craftiness will make sad work for conscience another day. If to do as we would be done by, be the law and the prophets; perverting the Scriptures, to injure the just in the work of the Lord, can be no branch of that law. *Ergo*, Who, then, is the Antinomian? I, who have levelled the Law's force at the sinner, or you, who have used it to slander the righteous?

" The believer having no more to do with the
" law than a woman with a dead husband, is black
" Antinomianism." If it be, I think my own experience and the Bible furnished me with it.

" Know you not, brethren, (for I speak to them
" that know the law) how that the law hath domi-
" nion over a man as long as he liveth? For the
" woman which hath an husband is bound by the
" law to her husband so long as he liveth, but if
" the husband be dead, she is loosed from the law
" of her husband. So then, if while her husband
" liveth she be married to another man, she shall
" be called an adulteress· but, if her husband be
" dead, *she is free from that law*, so that she is no
" adulteress, though she be married to another man.
" Wherefore, ye also are become dead to the law by

" the

body of Chriſt, [ye were crucified, and died in him;] that ye ſhould be married to another, " even to him who is raiſed from the dead, *that we* " *ſhould bring forth fruit unto God.*" Rom. Ch. vii.

The apoſtle here compares the Elect (before called) to a woman bound by the law to a huſband; which is binding, and cannot be diſſolved as long as either of the parties live. 2dly, That, if her huſband be dead, ſhe is free from that law, and may be married to another man: ſo the elect ſinner, who reckoned himſelf alive without the law in a ſtate of nature, finds that, when the commandment comes, ſin revives, and he dies. And, as ſoon as he is killed by the letter, or finds the law to be ordained unto death, *Rom.* vii. 10. he is become dead to the law; and the *law is* a killing letter, or *death, unto him,* for it *cannot give life.* He may then be married to Chriſt—not that he may live a looſe, licentious life, (for none but the Devil himſelf could ever father ſuch things upon a ſpiritual union with the Lord Jeſus Chriſt) but *that we ſhould bring forth fruit unto God,* which the killing power of the law could not enable us to do, becauſe it could not give life: *For, when we were in the fleſh, the motions of ſin, which were by the law, did work in our members, to bring forth fruit unto death,* Rom. vii. 5. The apoſtle tells us that we are dead to the law, looſed from the law, and delivered from it, and that by the body of Chriſt; for the law of the Spirit

C   of

of life in Chrift makes us free from the law of fin and death.

If all this be true—*that the believer is dead to the law*, as a widow is to the charms of a dead hufband, that the law can give him no more life than a dead hufband's corpfe can to a furviving widow; that, from this death, the widow is free from the law of her hufband, as the believer is from the law of Mofes; and that fhe may be married to another man, as the believer may to Chrift, and bear fruit to the fecond hufband, as the believer does to God; and be under the law of wedlock to the fecond hufband, as the believer is under the law [of eternal wedlock] to Chrift, who has made him free from the law of fin and death by the law of the Spirit of life, and brought him under grace, having efpoufed him to him for ever in righteoufnefs, in faithfulnefs, in loving-kindnefs, and in great mercy, that he may know his Lord and Hufband—I fay, fuch fouls can have no hufband but Chrift, nor be under any law but to him: and he gives us a fweet account of his eafy yoke in various terms, fuch as his *word*, his *law*, his *fayings*, his *commandments*, &c. which all amount to one and the fame thing, as we fhall fhew prefently.

God's law is written in his heart by the Spirit of the living God, which makes him a *living epiftle*, not a dead formalift. It is a *fountain of life*, not a killing letter; and it makes him fruitful to God,

not

not barren in the knowledge of him. The law, magnified and made honourable, is in the heart of Christ, and it is the law of the Spirit of life in him that makes the saint free; and he is under that law to Christ, whose WORD is life. *He that rejecteth me, and receiveth not my* WORDS, *hath one that judgeth him· the* WORD *that I have spoken, the same shall judge him in the last day.*—For I have not spoken of myself; but the Father which sent me, he gave me a COMMANDMENT, what I should say, and what I should speak; *and I know that his* COMMANDMENT *is life everlasting,* John XII. 48, 49, 50. He that hath my COMMANDMENTS, and keepeth them, he it is that loveth me. If a man love me, he will keep my WORDS, and my Father will love him. Verily verily, I say unto you, if a man keep my SAYING, *he shall never see death,* John viii 51. He that loveth me not, keepeth not my SAYINGS, *John* XIV. 24. This is the law of the Spirit of life, that the believer is under.

If ever my own lust should entice me to a loose and licentious way of living, the right horse shall wear the saddle: the Devil and William Huntington shall bear the scandal; for I will never palm it upon this doctrine, which has brought me from the drudgery of devils and the pains of hell, and has kept my soul in hope of heaven for now these sixteen years together: and, for my own part, I wish every one that calls me an Antinomian had got the same

hope.

C 2

hope.

hope. I think the devil would have more caufe to complain than he has now; and that lefs licentiouf-nefs, and more good works, would appear, than do at prefent, except in the talking part, or labour of the lip, which only brings a man to beggary. *In all labour there is profit, but the talk of the lip tendeth only to penury,* Prov. xiv. 23.

" A non-entity may be a rule as foon as love." Is this true, Sir? Is a non-entity, a thing that never had exiftence, as good a rule as *love, which is the fulfilling of the law?* Divine love, impreffed on the foul by the Spirit, is more valuable than the word *love* in the letter, or on tables of ftone. 'Tis love in the heart to God and our neighbour that is the *grand hinge* of all the law and the prophets, and a fulfilling of them, for it is both the old and the new commandment. But is it not ftrange that the word *love* in the letter fhould be the believer's only rule of life, and the Spirit of love in the heart be nothing but a non-entity? And is it not more ftrange, that he who holds the killing letter a rule of life, fhould be an evangelift; and he who holds that the righte-oufnefs of the law is fulfilled in thofe who walk in the Spirit, fhould be a black Antinomian? You will no more *live by your letter rule,* than you would by the word *bread* in the midft of famine. It is the *fubftance,* not the fhadow; the *thing,* not the name; the *power,* not the word, of him that is puffed up; the *life,* not the letter, God's own *work in the heart,*

not

not the talk of the lip, that God looks at; and that muſt ſave you, if ever you are ſaved. The will of God in the goſpel is a *perfect rule*. This myſtery of his will, which is the myſtery of faith, when revealed to the heart, and held in a pure conſcience, is the law of faith on the believer's mind and heart. Such a man is a ſpiritual man, and has a ſpiritual rule; is a new creature, and walks in newneſs of life; is guided by the Spirit of God, and ſerves in the new-neſs of the Spirit, not in the oldneſs of the letter. *In Chriſt Jeſus neither circumciſion availeth any thing, nor uncircumciſion, but a new creature: and as many as walk according to this rule, peace be on them, and mercy, and upon the Iſrael of God,* Gal. vi. 15.

Query. If the Law of Moſes, or Ten Commandments, be the believer's only rule of life, ſhould not a believer be ſaid to walk, to live, and to work, BY that rule? Does one text in the Book of God call the Pentateuch the believer's only rule? Or is there one text in that book which ſays that the believer is to walk, live, or work, BY that rule? Does not the Scripture ſay that he walks *by* faith, and lives *by* faith, and works *by* faith? On which account his obedience is called the obedience of faith, his life the life of faith, and his works the works of faith. And the law of faith muſt be a perfect rule, if whatſoever be not of faith is ſin.

Query 2. " They were both righteous before " God, walking IN all the commandments of the
" Lord

" Lord blamelefs." *Luke* i. 6. If they were both righteous, they were juftified by faith, *for he that believeth not is condemned.* And if they walked *in* God's commandments blamelefs, the commandments was the *way* they walked in, and faith was the *rule, by* which they walked in that *way.*

Pfalm cxix. 32. "I will run the *way* of thy com-
" mandments, when thou fhalt *enlarge* my heart."
Unbelief and flavifh fear contract the heart; faith, that worketh by love, enlarges it, love cafteth out fear. Then he that walks in love, (which you call a Non-entity) walks the *way* of God's commandments, though he be called a black Antinomian, for love is the fulfilling of the law, and he that lives and walks *by* faith, as his *rule,* is a righteous man, and walks *in* (though not *by*) God's commandments, blamelefs, though he be never fo much Limited.

I will keep my readers in *fufpence,* and my oppo-
nents *at bay,* no longer, but, for the comfort and eftablifhment of the former, and the confufion of the latter, I will put a few Queries· for hitherto fome have cried one thing, and fome another, the affemblies have been confufed, and the greater part have not known wherefore they came together, nor what they were come to hear. Paul fays, *We are not without law to God, but under the law to Chrift,* 1 Cor. ix 21. Here the believer *hes a law* to God, and is *under a law* to Chrift. Que, What law is
this

this that a believer *has*, and *holds*, toward God? Is it the law of Mofes, which worketh wrath? Is it the ten commandments, engraven on ftone, that minifter death? Is it the covenant of works, by which no flefh living can be juftified? Is it the killing letter, that ftops the mouth, and brings the world in guilty before God? If you reply, *Yes*, then, I fay, we are juft where we were; our faith is vain; we are yet in our fins, and Chrift profits us nothing. And if you fay, *No*, the believer is not without law to God, for he has his law in his heart, and holds a new covenant toward God; as it is written, " The days " come that I will make a *new covenant* with the " houfe of Ifrael, and the houfe of Judah; *not ac-* " *cording to the covenant* that I made with their fa- " thers when I took them out of the land of Egypt, " [they brake that] although I was a hufband unto " them But this fhall be the covenant that I will " make with the houfe of Ifrael after thofe days, " faith the Lord: I will put my law in their inward " part, and write it upon their heart; and I will be " their God, and they fhall be my people. And " they fhall all know me, from the leaft to the " greateft, faith the Lord; for I will forgive their " iniquity, and I will remember their fin no more." *Jer.* xxxi. 31, 32, 33, 34. I fay, if you allow this to be the law that the believer *has toward God*, you muft fay, as Paul does, we are delivered from [Mofes] law, that we may ferve in the newnefs of

the

the Spirit, and not in the oldnefs of the letter. Yea, you muft allow that the believer is not under the law, but under grace; for this law is the *law of faith*, and this covenant is the *covenant of grace:* and if you allow this to be the law that a believer hath toward God, (*who is not without law to him*) then what becomes of your only rule of life? yea, and you are as black an Antinomian as I. But if you reply, It is not this new covenant, it is not this law of faith in the heart, that the believer has and holds toward God, but the old covenant, or the killing letter—then I afk, What is that law that we are *redeemed* from, and *delivered* from, and are not *under?* What is that law that the child of Grace is not under? My opponents muft either make Chrift's redeeming us from under the law, his delivering us from the law, and his eafy yoke of grace, nothing, in order to hold their only rule; or elfe confefs themfelves Mofes's difciples altogether They muft either give up their rule, agree with Paul, and become rank Antinomians; or elfe drop their prefent title, and affume that of *minifters of the letter*, and hold their rule by virtue of that office. By the other they cannot; grace muft be no more grace, or work muft be no more work: they muft ftick to the law, and give up the Saviour's yoke; or ftand faft in Chrift, and give up the yoke of bondage.

"We

" We are under the law to Chrift," 1 *Cor.* ix. 21. Query, What law is this that the believer is under to Chrift? Is it your only rule of life? If fo, what is that law (as was before obferved) that Chrift delivered us, and faved us, from? And if you fay, *It is the law of the Spirit of life in Chrift Jefus,* (that the believer is under) *which makes him free from the law of fin and death,* Rom. viii. 2. then you agree with Paul, and fubmit to (what all my oppofers call) rank Antinomianifm: and where, then, is all that reproach to fall that has been heaped upon my head?

God has writ his law on the faint's heart, and put it in his mind; and this is the law of faith. therefore *he is not without law to God.* The law of the Spirit of life, in Chrift, makes him free from the law of fin and death, and *he is under this law to Chrift.* Bring any other yoke, or rule of life, from God's book, if you can. I defy every opponent I have to do it, or to bring one text to prove it. This law of the Spirit of life in Chrift goes by various names: it is the old commandment which is the *word,* and that is the *word of life.* It is called Chrift's Sayings, which is life He that *keepeth my faying fhall never fee death.* It is called the Law of the Wife, *which is a fountain of life;* the Law of Liberty, that makes us free from the law of death. It is called the Law of Truth, that was with Levi; the Law of Kindnefs, that comes from love, *that we may not die, but live.*

D   It

It is called the Law of Faith: *The juſt ſhall live by faith.* It is called Chriſt's Father's Commandment: *He gave me commandment what I ſhould ſay, and what I ſhould ſpeak, and I know that his commandment is life everlaſting.* Here is the Father's commandment, and here is the law of the Spirit of life in Chriſt. This is the law written in the mind, and put in the fleſhly tables of a broken heart, where it appears a fountain of life ſpringing up into life everlaſting; while your only rule, engraven on tables of ſtone, miniſters nothing but death.

Fighting againſt theſe things is only beating the air, and blowing the old trumpet is giving an uncertain ſound, for the watchman knows not what he ſays, nor whereof he affirms, and who can prepare for the battle, in hope of gaining the victory, when it is not the fight of faith that they are called to engage in?

" Faith is an eye, a hand, a leg—Ergo, no rule."

Anſwer. The law of faith includes, and affords, every thing that the law of Moſes requires. And it is a perfect rule; for whatſoever the law of faith doth not point out, and whatſoever is not done in the faith of the goſpel, is ſin. If it be no rule of obedience, how can the ſaint's obedience be called the obedience of faith? And how can men be puniſhed with everlaſting deſtruction for not obeying it, and be condemned as hypocrites and unbeliev-

ers,

ers, if it be not a rule of obedience?   It appears to
me, that it is both a *rule of life* and a *rule of judgment.*
The Scripture fays, we are to walk *by* faith, and live
by faith.   How can a man walk by it, and live by it,
if it is no rule?   The law of faith is a perfect rule,
and the grace of faith directs the fteps of the faints
to walk by it.   Nor is the law of Mofes, or ten
commandments, ever called the believer's only rule
of life or walk; nor is the believer ever faid to walk
by the law of Mofes, or *by* the ten commandments.
A believer is faid to walk by faith; and a juft man
to walk *in* the commandments, not *by* them; and to
run the *way* of them : and without faith there is no
walking *in* thefe commandments, and, without love
to enlarge the heart, there is no running the *way* of
them; and both faith and love belong to the perfect
rule that I contend for.

" The Law is perfect—and eternal."

Both thefe are true: and, had you feen the perfection of it, and felt it's force, you would have
called it, as others have done, a yoke that neither
faint nor finner is able to bear; and would have been
glad to have found it magnified by, and fecured in
the heart of, a Mediator, rather than contend and
defire to have your neck brought under it.

" Angels are under it."

Is this fpeaking as the oracles of God?   The
law was delivered by God himfelf to Adam, and by

Mofes

Mofes it was delivered to Ifrael, and it was ordained by angels in the hand of a Mediator. But I never read that it was delivered *to* angels; nor were they ever circumcifed to become debtors to fulfil it, nor is there one infpired penman in the Bible that ever applied it to them. God's voice by them is to the fons of men, nor did I ever hear of any modern divine applying it to them, till Sir Ham Cottifh and Mr. Wake appeared in orders. If angels are under any law, I think they are under the *perfect law of liberty*, or what Solomon calls the *law of kindnefs.* 'Tis their liberty that makes their fervice perfect freedom, and it is the law of loving-kindnefs that makes them fly fo fwift as they do, and cover their faces and their feet, when they have done, in token of no boafting of merit: the glory is given to the Object they cry to—Holy, holy, holy—Holy Father, Holy Son, and Holy Ghoft. This law of liberty and love none but the real faint knows, and is moft certainly the law of angels, and will be enjoyed in perfection by glorified faints when they come to be *equal to the angels of God,* being the children of the Refurrection.

In thefe matters is manifefted the children of the bond woman and the children of the free—the minifters of the letter, and the minifters of the Spirit. The minifter that hath this new covenant made with him, and this law of faith written on his heart; who is made free from the law of fin and death by the

law

law of the Spirit of life in Chrift Jefus; is a minifter of God's Spirit, *not of the letter*. He is an ambaffador of Chrift, and an ambaffador of peace. He is an adopted fon of God, and the Spirit of his heavenly Father fpeaketh in him. He is, according to the troubled finner's wifh, in God's ftead. He takes forth the vile from the precious, *and is as God's mouth*. He has the *Spirit* and *word* of God, the *keys of the kingdom of heaven*. What his miniftry binds upon earth, *in heaven is bound*, and what fuch a miniftry loofes on earth, *in heaven is loofed*. Chrift is with fuch always, *even to the end of the world*. The gofpel is the miniftration of the Spirit to the end of time; and Chrift is the fame yefterday, to-day, and for ever. As *Chrift was, fo* are fuch minifters *in the world*. He that receives them, receives Chrift, for he dwells in their hearts by faith, and is in them the hope of glory; and they who defpife them, defpife Chrift that fent them, and his Father, who fent him. *They have power to fhut heaven, that it rain not during their prophecy*; for there can be no benediction from Heaven *but by the miniftry of the Spirit. They have power to turn waters to blood as often as they will.* Sinners, compared to water, muft die in their fins, and in their blood, if they *do defpite to the Spirit of grace*, or quench the Spirit in the Lord's ambaffadors. And this power is not of them, *they have this treafure in earthen veffels, that the excellency and the power may appear to be of God,*

and

and not of them. Such men come not with excellency of fpeech, or men's wifdom, but in the demonftration of the Spirit, and with power: not with the words that man teacheth, but with fuch as the Holy Ghoft teacheth; not comparing themfelves with themfelves, but comparing fpiritual things with fpiritual, appealing to every man's confcience in the fight of God, not knowing the fpeech of them that are puffed up, but the power; declaring that the kingdom of heaven ftandeth not in word, but in power, and that a faint's faith ftands not in the wifdom of men, but in the power of God. And who will make me a liar in this, and prove my fpeech to be nothing worth?

It is the bleffed Spirit of God that *teftifies of Chrift to us, and glorifies him in us,* and it is in fpirit and in truth that he will be *honoured in us,* and *worfhipped by us.* Nor do I believe that God pays any regard to any one's vindicating his honour or his truth, but his own fpiritual children; *not allowing a hypocrite to take his covenant in his mouth, or even to declare his ftatutes, nor to offer a facrifice without committing abomination.*

When I firft came to London, I heard ftrange things held forth for doctrines. but I knew that *I was young, and durft not fhew mine opinion,* for I thought that *days fhou'd fpeak, and that the multitude of years fhould teach wifdom.* But I find, now, that old men are not always wife, nor do the aged under-
fland

stand judgment *Man muſt fetch his knowledge from afar, and aſcribe righteouſneſs to his Maker,* if he does any good. It is the breath of God that gives a man life, and the inſpiration of the Almighty that gives him underſtanding. Without this, a man reaſons with unprofitable talk, and with words, or ſpeeches, wherewith he can do no good. His converſation and arguments are blunt; and, if he cannot *whet the edge with prayer, he muſt put forth more ſtrength,* Ecclef. x. 10. But *by ſtrength ſhall no man prevail,* 1 Sam. ii. 9. When the *poor and needy,* in *ſpirit,* ſpeak right, *how forcible are right words!* But converſation, or argument, from a barren heart and a crafty head, are, *like the white of an egg,* unſavoury, and without a concluſion; and what doth their arguings prove, diſprove, or reprove?

An unconverted man is no miniſter of the goſpel; an uninſpired man is no miniſter of the Spirit. An unbeliever cannot preach the faith of God's elect; he is not endued with power from on high; nor is there either excellency or power with him. Caſting out devils is not converſion: the devil muſt be *caſt out* of the heart, and *Chriſt formed in it,* before a man can be converted to the faith of Jeſus. Such are no preachers of the kingdom of God, *for that is not in word.* Such can ſay no more than Judas could, *that they have taken part of the miniſtry,* the *office* of a miniſter, not the ſpirit of the miniſtry; and ſuch are ſure to make *ſhipwreck* of their ſyſtem of faith,

for

for *a prating fool shall fall, and another shall take his office.* The best titles that the word of God gives to uninspired men, are—*Wells without water,* boasters *of a false gift, clouds without rain, virgins without oil, instruments without life,* trumpeters without *any certain sound, beaters of the air, runners at uncertainty, cutters, wolfs, creepers into houses, haters of those that are good, vain janglers, ministers of the letter, deceitful workers, and false apostles.* These are the best titles that men can claim from Scripture, who are *sensual, destitute of the Spirit,* and who *have not the doctrine of Christ,* for such have not God. And it is clear that the children of God and the children of the devil divide the whole world   the bond woman's bastards, and the free woman's sons; the ministers of the letter, and those of the Spirit; impostors of Satan, and ambassadors of Christ, goats and sheep; serpents and doves; children of the flesh, and children of promise, reprobates and chosen vessels; divide the human race. Nor is it in the power of either devils or hypocrites to break down this middle wall of partition, so as to lay the garden of Eden and the dreary desart together. The Church will ever remain to be God's husbandry, God's family, and God's building ——A few learned and weighty sentences discharged against this doctrine, at different times, with a few Queries on them.

“ The

" *The daring Antinomian, who denies the law to be*
" *a rule of life, does despite to the Spirit of grace.*"
Query—How can a man who levels the force of the
whole law at ministers of the letter and bond-
children, (*to whom the law speaks;*) and enforces,
and insists upon, a spiritual birth, spiritual worship,
a spiritual life and walk, a deliverance from dead
works and lip-service, and a service of freedom in
the newness of the Spirit; and who declares that,
without holiness in heart and life by the Spirit of
Christ, that a man is no more than a hypocrite—
do despite to the Spirit of grace? I think, if such a
man does *despite* to any, it must be to a dead forma-
list, and his dead works performed *in the oldness of*
the letter.

" *Let no man exalt Jesus at the expence of Moses.*"
Query—Is there any other way of establishing the
honour of Moses as a faithful servant, or his law as
a revelation of wrath, than by the righteousness of
faith, which was witnessed both by the law and the
prophets? If we would imitate Moses in faithful-
ness, must we not ascribe greatness to our God,
seeing he is the Rock, and his work is perfect, and
there is none like the God of Jeshurun, who rideth
upon the heavens in our help, and in his excellency
on the sky? And say to all those who cleave to
the *old veil,* as Moses did, that they are blind, and
destitute of faith; a nation void of counsel, *children*
in whom is no faith? " I have led you forty years

E

" in

" in this wildernefs; *and God has not given you eyes*
" *to fee, nor ears to hear, nor hearts to underftand,*
" *to this day."* Does afcribing the whole of our
falvation to the grace of God difhonour Mofes,
who has curfed, and ftill accufes every foul that
breaks his law, and yet cleaves to it for life? Or is
there any other way of exalting Mofes, or ourfelves,
(as God's fervants) but by bowing down the mean
man, humbling the haughty, and exalting the Lord
of Hofts alone, feeing he only is to be exalted in
gofpel days? *They that honour me, will I honour;*
but thofe that defpife me fhall be lightly efteemed.

" *The only rule of life is included in the law."*
Query—Can you point the faith of our Lord Jefus
Chrift, repentance toward God, juftification by,
imputation, regeneration by the Spirit, worfhipping
the Trinity in fpirit and in truth, felf-denial, a daily
crofs, walking in newnefs of life, ferving in the
newnefs of the Spirit, and going to God by a new
and living Way which he hath confecrated through
the veil of Chrift's flefh: I fay, can thefe things be
made plain from the ten commandments? Does
God promife to give grace and glory in or by that
difpenfation? Or is the *fhining path of the juft* dif-
covered by *blacknefs and darknefs;* or by looking
with open face, and beholding, as in a glafs, the
glory of God in the face of Jefus Chrift?

" *I would*

" *I would as soon let the Pope get into my pulpit,*
" *as a man that says the law is not a rule of life.*"
Query—Would you not, then, exclude the Saviour,
and all his apostles, from your pulpit; and all the
ministers of the Spirit who speak as the oracles of
God? Do any of these send the believer to the law
of Moses for their only rule to live, to walk, and to
work by? Would not this doctrine have kept them
halting between two opinions? Can the believer's
thoughts be established by this? Has not God di-
vided the world into two classes, children of the
flesh, and children of the promise? Are not the
children of the flesh under the law, and those of the
promise under grace? If the law speaks only to
those who are under the law, does not the gospel
speak to the heirs of promise, who are under grace?
If the law is a rule of life to the bond child, *This do,
and thou shalt live;* is not the law of faith the believer's rule, seeing he that *believes has life,* and
shall *never die;* and as many as walk according to
this *rule,* mercy on them, and peace, and upon the
Israel of God? Is there any thing that the law requires which the promise does not give? Is there
any thing by God's *commanding will* required, that
his *will of promise,* called *the good pleasure of his will,*
does not work in us? Does God's *willingness to
shew his wrath on the vessels of wrath fitted for de-
struction,* as revealed in *thick darkness,* bring any
better tidings to sinners ears than the *good-will of*

E 2

him

him that once dwelt in the bush, and who has since proclaimed from heaven, by his angels, glory to himself in the highest, on earth peace, and *good-will towards men* in the law of faith? The law of faith respects all, implies all, includes all, and fulfils all. There is nothing revealed in the law that faith is not obedient to; there is nothing required in the law that the law of faith doth not furnish the believer with. God's *will of commandments* reveals him WILLING *to shew his wrath, and make his power known, endured with much long-suffering, on the vessels of wrath*, Rom. ix. 22. *But this is the* WILL *of him that sent me*, (says the Saviour) *that whosoever seeth the Son, and believeth on him, may not perish, but have everlasting life*—for it is not the WILL of our Father, which is in heaven, that one of these little ones (in faith) should perish. Here is God's *will*, and my *rule*; and it may truly be called *the believer's only rule of life*, for *life everlasting* accompanies this *rule*, and all who walk according to it.

" *We have got some in our day who say the law is*
" *not a rule of life. For my part, I know not how*
" *such men read their Bibles: I read that, without*
" *holiness, no man shall see the Lord.*" Query—But does holiness come by the law? Are we sanctified thereby? Those who stick to the law are clean in their own eyes, but, are they washed from their filthiness? They justify themselves; but, are they

just

juft before God? Can they be holy without being fanctified by the Holy Ghoft? *And he that minifters the Spirit, doth he it by the works of the law, or by the hearing of faith?* Is not the Holy Ghoft the Spirit of promife? Does he go forth from Mount Sinai, or Mount Zion? Does he come by the law, or by the gofpel? Are any cleanfed but by the Saviour's blood? Is there any heart purified but by faith? Is it not by the *exceeding great and precious promifes that we are made partakers of the divine nature?* Are not the fons of God made partakers of the Spirit of Adoption? Does not God *chaften fuch for their profit, that they may be partakers of his holinefs?* And does not this all come from the " ministration of the Spirit, which exceeds in glory? " For the ministration of death had no glory in this " refpect, by reafon of the glory that excelleth; for " if that which is done away was glorious, much " more that which remaineth is glorious." 2 *Cor.* ix. 8, 9, 10, 11.

Thefe are fome of the weighty fentences which have at different times been thrown out againft me, and the doctrine that God himfelf hath taught me. And it is evident that they have confuted nothing, cleared nothing; nor hath any thing been eftablifhed by this buffoonery; nor ever will, for Truth hath declared, that *thofe who turn afide to vain jangling, defiring to be teachers of the law, know not what they*

fay,

say, nor whereof they affirm, and this chain of quotations is a sufficient proof of it   I shall now leave the prieft, and fpeak to the people, or, drop a word to the reader.

COURTEOUS AND CHRISTIAN READER,

I Little thought that, for dropping a fingle sentence from the pulpit, I fhould have been loaded with fo much reproach, and have been led forth into fo long a controverfy; but we read of fome *who make a man an offender for a word*, even when *the poor and needy fpeaketh right*.   But, blefled be God, all that has been written or faid has never in the leaft brought my mind over to long for *Padan-aram*, the land of *Egypt*, or for a fecond journey through the *Wildernefs of Sin*.   *My face is ftill toward Mount Gilead*, the *land of Canaan*, and *Mount Zion*, fo beautiful for fituation, hence called the joy of the whole earth   for I am perfuaded that thefe are ftill in my road; knowing that moft who are faved fhall view the houfe of Ifaac, fee the land that is very far off, and *enquire the way to Zion with their faces thitherward*.

I have as yet feen nothing in the writings, nor heard any thing from the pulpit, nor feen any thing in the life of my opponents, that has in the leaft influenced my mind to incline toward the yoke of bondage, but quite the reverfe; and I blefs God that

he

he has not in the least permitted my soul to wander from the truth, in order to follow them in stumbling *upon the dark mountains*; but, contrariwise, all that they have said has drove me closer to Christ, and farther and farther into the mystery of faith. And I do in reality believe, that this controversy has been intended (under God) to make me search the covenant of grace more closely, and to bring forth those truths which are so contrary to flesh and blood, and so despicable in the eyes of the unconverted. And I must confess that I am greatly indebted to my numerous opposers for their close pursuit of me; for, had they let me alone, I never had, in this my pilgrimage, seen the beauty of the everlasting covenant, as I now see it, nor the rich displays of grace, as they now appear, especially in the muddy glass of my opponents ignorance.

The law of God, so often mentioned in holy writ as written on the hearts of his chosen people, is the covenant of grace, the mystery of faith, the new covenant, or the everlasting gospel, which is so little understood in this our day; and all the happy partakers thereof are *under the grace of God, which shall reign, through righteousness, to eternal life, by Jesus Christ our Lord.*

There are five things, reader, which will make thee and me fruitful, and acceptable, even when it shall be made manifest that the kingdom of God is

not

not in word; and that is—a union with the true and
living Vine; a confidence in the blood and righteoufnefs of the Saviour; the dominion of grace
reigning through righteoufnefs; the promife of
God that *we fhall bring forth fruit in old age*; and
the certainty of *the Holy Ghoft abiding with us for
ever.*

Alfo, take no heed, reader, unto all the words that
are fpoken, *Ecclef.* vii. 21. for a vain jangler utters
diverfe vanities: but fearch the Scriptures for thy-
felf; and they will inform thee concerning the two
covenants, (that of grace, and that of works;) God's
WILL *(of commandments)* and his WILL *(of promife.)*
GOD's WILL is man's *rule:* the former is a *rule* for
(the *fervant*, and the *flave*; the latter is a *rule* for the
(*fon*, and the *heir*). The fervant muft work and walk
by the former, in order to get his wages, (which is
reckoned of debt,) for it is the *will of God* that he
fhould *do thofe things, if he will enter into life.* The
latter is *God's good-will* to the fon; and the *penitent
fon that obeyed, and went into the vineyard, did the*
WILL *of his father*, Matt. xxi. 31. *For whofoever
fhall do the* WILL *of my Father, which is in heaven,*
(faith Chrift) *the fame is my mother, and fifter, and
brother,* Matt. xii. 50.

To the fervant God calls himfelf a Mafter; but
to the fon he calls himfelf a Father. *A fon honour-
eth his* FATHER, *and a fervant his* MASTER. *If,
then,*

then, I be a Father, where is mine honour? and if I be a Master, where is my fear? saith the Lord of Hosts. Mal. i. 6. If this be the case, reader, is not the *Master's will* the servant's *rule?* Let the Master's *commanding will* be resisted, or not obeyed or complied with, the place is lost, and the wages too, *for the servant abideth not in the house ever, but the son abideth ever.* And is not the GOOD WILL of the father the son's *rule,* as hath been before proved; which is called *our heavenly Father's will;* his *good will;* the *mystery of the Father's will, made known; the good pleasure of his will,* which he fulfils in us, and the work of faith with power? *Henceforth Christ calls us not servants, for the servant knoweth not what his Lord doth; but I have called you friends, for all things that I have heard of the Father I have made known unto you,* John xv 15. Thou seest, reader, that the servant knows not this *mystery of our heavenly Father's* WILL: he is not acquainted with this *rule,* only sons and friends are entrusted with these secrets, *God's secret is with them that fear him,* and them only; *and he shews them his covenant.*

It is for want of knowledge in this mystery that thou hearest so much cavilling for the law being the only rule of life. They may have some knowledge of it literally and grammatically, but not spiritually nor experimentally. *The natural man discerns not the things of the Spirit,* nor does he know the power:

F

therefore

therefore they do err, not knowing the Scriptures,
(which are fpiritual) *nor the power of God.* If the
law of Mofes be the believer's *only* RULE *of life,*
the gofpel has no rule at all: fo they make God's
good-will, which is the *law of faith,* a mere nothing, *and fo the life, walk, and work* of faith, is
no obedience at all, for there is neither *will, law,*
nor *rule,* to be obeyed. " Surely thefe good men
" do not exalt Jefus at the expence of Mofes," but
they exalt Mofes at the expence of Jefus: for our
King, Sovereign, Lawgiver, and Ruler, has left us
no rule to live by; though the man that does the
will of our Father which is in heaven fhall enter
into his kingdom; while the fervant that comes with
" Lord! Lord! open to us!" fhall be fhut out

Chrift's voice is to his fheep, and everlafting life
attends it. His fheep hear his voice, and follow
him; and fuch fhall enter into life, for he is the
way, the truth, and the life On the other hand,
whatfoever the law faith, it faith to them that are
under it: and this way to heaven by works feems
right unto a man, but the end thereof are the ways
of death. This is not the voice of Chrift, but the
voice of words: nor is it the new and living Way
that God has confecrated, but the contrary. Nor
is the old cry, " *The law is the only rule of life,*"
Chrift's voice, nor any thing like it, it belongs to
the old wives fables, not to the lively oracles of
God by Chrift Jefus.

Satan

Satan has gained a deal of ground by the repeated cry—" The law is the only rule of a believer's life." It has served to keep many seeking sinners in chains; and to blind some discerning people, who have been so hoodwinked by the old veil, that a little dry morality will suffice. It has armed legions of light, trifling professors, with malice, and matter for slander, so that, as soon as a gospel minister brings forth the mystery of faith, it is blasphemed, and loaded with the name of black Antinomianism, and the preacher of it is viewed as first cousin to Simon Magus. By these means the bond-servant keeps the pulpit, and the devil the palace; for Satan knows there is no fear of truth gaining ground upon the heart and affections while it is ridiculed and blasphemed. If this is not rebelling against the light, and doing despite to the Spirit of grace, what is? The gospel is set forth as having no sufficient rule, Christ as divested of his sovereignty, the old law as the better covenant, and Moses as worthy of more honour than Jesus : his ambassadors are represented as encouragers of vice, and the truths of the everlasting gospel as leading to licentiousness—and what can the devil himself do or say more?

I have in this little piece endeavoured to furnish thee, reader, with a few arguments, that thou mayest have somewhat to answer them that glory in appear-

ance,

therefore they do err, not knowing the Scriptures, (which are spiritual) *nor the power of God.* If the law of Moses be the believer's *only* RULE *of life,* the gospel has no rule at all· so they make God's *good-will,* which is the *law of faith,* a mere nothing, and so the life, walk, and work of faith, is no obedience at all, for there is neither *will, law,* nor *rule,* to be obeyed. " Surely these good men " do not exalt Jefus at the expence of Mofes," but they exalt Moses at the expence of Jefus: for our King, Sovereign, Lawgiver, and Ruler, has left us no rule to live by; though the man that does the will of our Father which is in heaven shall enter into his kingdom, while the servant that comes with " Lord! Lord! open to us!" shall be shut out

Chrift's voice is to his sheep, and everlasting life attends it. His sheep hear his voice, and follow him, and such shall enter into life, for he is the way, the truth, and the life. On the other hand, whatsoever the law saith, it saith to them that are under it: and this way to heaven by works seems right unto a man, but the end thereof are the ways of death. This is not the voice of Christ, but the *voice of words:* nor is it the new and living Way that God has consecrated, but the contrary. Nor is the old cry, " *The law is the only rule of life,"* Chrift's voice, nor any thing like it, it belongs to the old wives fables, not to the lively oracles of God by Chrift Jesus.

Satan

Satan has gained a deal of ground by the repeated cry—" The law is the only rule of a believer's life." It has ferved to keep many feeking finners in chains; and to blind fome difcerning people, who have been fo hoodwinked by the old veil, that a little dry morality will fuffice. It has armed legions of light, trifling profeffors, with malice, and matter for flander; fo that, as foon as a gofpel minifter brings forth the myftery of faith, it is blafphemed, and loaded with the name of black Antinomianifm; and the preacher of it is viewed as firft coufin to Simon Magus. By thefe means the bond-fervant keeps the pulpit, and the devil the palace; for Satan knows there is no fear of truth gaining ground upon the heart and affections while it is ridiculed and blafphemed. If this is not rebelling againft the light, and doing defpite to the Spirit of grace, what is? The gofpel is fet forth as having no fuffi-cient rule, Chrift as divefted of his fovereignty, the old law as the better covenant, and Mofes as worthy of more honour than Jefus: his ambaffadors are reprefented as encouragers of vice, and the truths of the everlafting gofpel as leading to licentiouf-nefs—and what can the devil himfelf do or fay more?

I have in this little piece endeavoured to furnifh thee, reader, with a few arguments, that thou mayeft have f mewhat to anfwer them that glory in appear-

ance,

ance, but not in heart. Love thou the truth, and peace: and be not difmayed and terrified at every minifter of confufion; fuch muft come, but God will bring every work into judgment. If a preacher holds not the myftery of faith in a pure confcience, you know he has nothing to recommend him to the excellent of the earth: fuch always will be battering the middle wall, and warping to the flefh, and to the law, contending for no other holinefs than a fair fhew in the flefh, an outward reformation, dealing in general terms, drawing no line between the elect and reprobate, faint and finner; obfcuring the great truths of the gofpel, dealing in invitations; fpeaking well of the erroneous, and ridiculing the juft, aiming to affect and move the paffions; coveting the name and applaufe of a gentleman of cand.d and liberal fentiments, and giving up nine doctrines of the Bible out of ten in order to gain it. But this is not rightly dividing the word of truth, nor doing the work of an evangelift; no real converfion work goes on here, God fets not his feal to this, this is not taking forth the vile from the precious, nor being valiant for truth; it is walking in craftinefs, and handling the word of God deceitfully, and fo it will appear when the great and terrible day of the Lord comes, in which *he will render his anger with fury, and his rebukes with flames of fire,* Ifa. lxvi. 15. The canting applaufe

of

of hypocrites will be no fhelter from that ftorm, nor armour proof fufficient to repel the force of thofe flames.

Take heed how, and what you hear, and, if a man hath not the doctrine of Chrift, Truth declares that he hath not God: receive him not, neither into your heart, nor into your houfe, nor bid him God fpeed. Let others juftify him, and carefs him, as they may; be not thou a partaker of other men's fins; nor entail his evil deeds on thy head, by wifh-ing him fuccefs.

Prize your liberty, and ftand faft in it. If thou art a fon of the free woman, with a great fum thou didft obtain this freedom——freedo n from the bondage and curfe of the law, freedom from the reigning and deftroying power of fin; freedom of accefs to a throne of grace, freedom to call God Father; freedom of fpeech, and freedom of foul. Truth hath made thee free, therefore love the truth; the Spirit hath made thee free, therefore walk in the Spirit; Chrift hath made thee free, and thou art free indeed. And may God blefs thee with the joys of his falvation, and uphold thee with his free Spirit; and then thou wilt fay with truth and wifdom, what many have uttered in falfhood and ignorance, namely, that *God's fervice is perfect freedom.*

But, if thou once turn thy back upon the truth, thou haft neither fhield nor buckler. He who keeps

the

the word of Chrift's patience fhall be kept from the hour of temptation. He that erreth from the way of underftanding fhall remain in the congregation of the dead. The prudent are crowned with knowledge, and they muft hold faft that which they have, that no man take their crown. It is not candour that fecures the prize, but faithfulnefs. *Be thou faithful unto death, and I will give thee a crown of life,* Rev. ii. 10.

The fon and heir is not to be debafed, nor reduced to a level with the baftard and the flave, nor is the fervant to be exalted to a footing with the fon. The fon, who is lord of all, differs much from him: for he is not now under tutors and governors, for the time appointed of the Father is come, and the Spirit of adoption is given, *Gal.* iv. 2, 6. The fon is not to wear the fervant's yoke, nor is the eafy yoke of the fon to be applied to the fervant. This is not rightly dividing the word. *God hath mercy on whom he WILL have mercy;* and this *will* of mercy is the *good-will* of God in Chrift concerning his fons and daughters; it is the heavenly Father's will revealed, and is our rule. *I will,* and *you fhall,* runs through the whole myftery of faith: it is his *will* of purpofe, and his *will* of promife, and is the faint's perfect, unalterable, and eternal rule of life, walk, and converfation.

And

And whom [God] WILL *he hardeneth.* This is his *will of commandments,* by which he WILL by no means clear the guilty, but WILL make his power known on the veffels of wrath. This *will* never humbled or foftened any finner, (nor does his *good-will* ever *harden* any) This is the fervant's rule of life, and rule of work for life, by which none can ever live: *Wherfore I gave them alfo* STATUTES *that were not good, and* JUDGMENTS WHEREBY THEY SHOULD NOT LIVE *Ezek.* xx 25.

When my opponents can make God's *will of promife* and his *will of commandments,* his *good-will* in Chrift and his *will of difpleafure* in the law, his *will of mercy* and his *will of judgment,* the Saviour's eafy yoke and Mofes' unbearable yoke, the covenant of grace and that of works, the killing letter and the quickening Spirit, to be one and the fame thing—then the elect and reprobate, the child of God and the child of the Devil, are made one alfo. And, when this is done, all my *rank Antinomianifm* is confuted, and fcattered into all winds ——Which is juft as eafy to be done, as to unite the two poles; bring Chrift and Belial, the family of heaven and hell, together: God's good-will fixes the one in heaven, and his will of judgment fixes the other in hell.

Reader,

Reader, fare thee well. Grace, mercy, and peace, be with thee.—And, when it is well with thee, remember me in prayer, *That I may speak of the glory of Chrift's kingdom, and talk of the power, to make known unto the fons of men his mighty acts, and the glorious majefty of his kingdom,* Pfal. cxlv. 11, 12.—and thou wilt greatly oblige thy willing fervant, in the kingdom and patience of Chrift,

WM. HUNTINGTON, S. S.

P. S. When the laft piece on this fubject appeared in the world, two young men, fearing to read it, laid it before God, and entreated him to convince them whether it contained the truth or not, that they might either embrace or reject it, and, after earneft prayer, they ventured to look into it, but proceeded with caution, as a man would over a bog. As God would have it, neither of them tumbled in; but they plunged, out of their bondage, into that love, peace, and liberty, which they never enjoyed before.— I wifh every reader of this pamphlet would go and do likewife. There are no better appeals than thofe which are made to the Searcher of hearts, nor is there any fear of falfe or evafive anfwers from a throne of grace: a trial there is fure to difcover the rottennefs or foundnefs of the author.

9 N064

Reader, fare thee well. Grace, mercy, and peace, be with thee —And, when it is well with thee, remember me in prayer, *That I may speak of the glory of Chrift's kingdom, and talk of the power; to make known unto the fons of men his mighty acts, and the glorious majefty of his kingdom*, Pfal. cxlv. 11, 12 — and thou wilt greatly oblige thy willing fervant, in the kingdom and patience of Chrift,

WM. HUNTINGTON, S. S.

———————

P. S.   When the laft piece on this fubject appeared in the world, two young men, fearing to read it, laid it before God, and entreated him to convince them whether it contained the truth or not, that they might either embrace or reject it, and, after earneft prayer, they ventured to look into it, but proceeded with caution, as a man would over a bog.   As God would have it, neither of them tumbled in, but they plunged, out of their bondage, into that love, peace, and liberty, which they never enjoyed before.— I wifh every reader of this pamphlet would go and do likewife.   There are no better appeals than thofe which are made to the Searcher of hearts, nor is there any fear of falfe or evafive anfwers from a throne of grace. a trial there is fure to difcover the rottennefs or foundnefs of the author.

9 NO64

CPSIA information can be obtained at www.ICGtesting.com
Printed in the USA
LVOW122100070612

285194LV00003B/63/P